Deliverance

OF THE

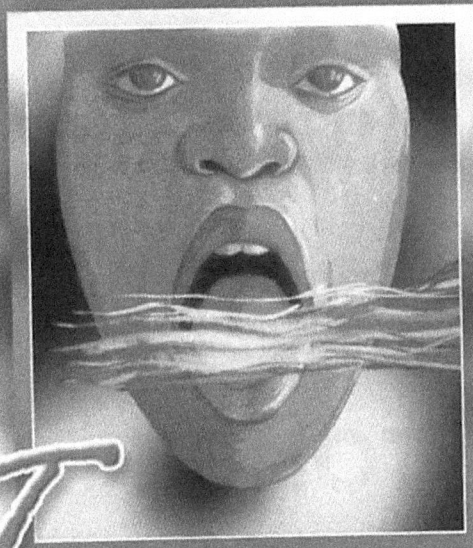

Tongue

DR. D. K. OLUKOYA

DELIVERANCE

OF THE

TONGUE

Dr. D.K Olukoya

© 2009 A.D. – DELIVERANCE OF THE TONGUE
Dr. D.K. Olukoya
ISBN: 978-8021- 98 -0
A Publication of
TRACTS AND PUBLICATIONS GROUP
MOUNTAIN OF FIRE AND MIRACLES MINISTRIES
13, Olasimbo Street, off Olumo Road, (By UNILAG Second
Gate), Onike, Iwaya.
P.O.Box 2990, Sabo, Yaba, Lagos, Nigeria. 08087770111,
08087770112, 08087700111, 08087700115
Website: www.mountain-of-fire.com
E-mail: mfmhqworldwide@mountainoffire.org

I salute my wonderful wife, Pastor Shade, for her invaluable
support in the ministry.

I appreciate her unquantifiable support in the book ministry as
the cover designer, art editor and art advisor.

First Edition

i

TABLE OF CONTENTS

I believe that you have not picked up this publication to waste your time. You are reading it because you want to drink from the well of salvation. It is necessary that we consider the subject of the deliverance of the tongue because the tongue can be a source of problem and at the same time a source of blessings. The tongue has destroyed many lives and also, it has improved and blessed the lives of many people. Let us start by looking at the general definition of deliverance.

GENERAL DEFINITION OF DELIVERANCE

1. Deliverance can be generally defined as release from captivity, slavery or

oppression. This release could involve many things such as the following:

a. Casting out a demon from a place, a person, or a thing. This means that demons can possess a person, a place or an inanimate object.

b. Breaking of curses, spells and bewitchment.

c. Breaking of evil yokes.

d. Loosing the bands of wickedness.

e. Breaking evil covenants, contracts or promissory notes of the enemy.

f. Spiritual cleansing from evil marks.

g. Removal of satanic loads and burdens.

h. Uprooting evil seeds.

i. Breaking of bondage.

j.   Removal of satanic embargo.

k.   Destroying the works of darkness.

A lot of people have a wrong idea of what deliverance is. Whenever people hear of deliverance, they usually associate it with getting delivered from witches and wizards. This is just a part of deliverance. By these definitions and descriptions, you should now understand the term, deliverance.

THE TONGUE

When God created man in the beginning, He gave man a lot of powers. God gave man the power of imagination and power to dominate and subdue the earth. For example, no matter how dangerous an animal is, when it sees a human being, it initially gets afraid before gathering courage to attack. One of the powers God gave to man is the power of spoken word and the reason why a lot of people are in bondage can be traced to their tongue. Many tongues are under bondage. The book of James, Chapter 1 verse 26 tells us that as far as any one is unable to control his or her tongue, such a person's religion is in vain. Also, chapter 3 of James, verse 2 to 12 also tells us that when a man is able to control his tongue, he will also be able to control the rest of his body. The passage also tells us that the tongue is a little member that boasts of great things. It also describes the tongue as a fire. When fire is controlled, it can be very useful to mankind, but when it becomes uncontrollable, it can be a very dangerous destroyer.

The tongue is also described as a world of iniquity that defiles the whole body. This means that this little member can put the whole body in bondage. It is humanly impossible to tame the tongue or put it under control, like we do with wild animals such as lions, horses e.t.c. The tongue is an unruly evil. It is used to bless God and curse men, and it is full of deadly poison. It is capable of good conversation as well as bitter strife. Although, it is a small member of the body, the Bible says, it can ignite a big flame. The tongue has destroyed families, countries and nations. It is a dangerous member of the body. God gave man two eyes, two nostrils, two ears, but one mouth containing one big fish; the tongue. The tongue can be used to serve God or serve the devil. At the same time, the tongue is one of the most effective passports to hell fire. That is why Jesus said, "For by thy words thou shalt be justified, and by thy words thou shalt be condemned" (Matthew 12:37). Every man will give account of every idle word that he speaks on the Day of Judgment. If you do not control your tongue, it will end up controlling you. Many lives would have been so sweet, if at one stage in their lives, they were dumb like Zachariah and did not utter a word. A lot of people will not be where they are now if they had not engaged in a particular conversation. To make it worse, there are demons living on people's tongues. And the Bible says if you cannot control your tongue you will not be able to discipline other parts of your body. When your tongue is under the control of God, you will speak God's words, but when it is under the control of devil and demons, you may speak God's words for a little while, but will eventually speak the devil's words. Be assured that the words you speak will shape your life. As little as your tongue is, it shapes your life. Your present life today is as a result of what you have been saying yesterday with your mouth. This is why the Bible says that death and life are in the power of the tongue. The tongue can kill and it can make alive.

God gave us seven openings on the head, and the seventh one needs to be controlled. If you open your mouth more than the other openings, which are two ears, two eyes and two nostrils, it will surely get you into trouble. God gave us only one mouth so that when others are opened twice, it is opened only once, that is, see twice, speak once, hear twice, speak once etc. There is nothing so great and powerful that the tongue cannot control because it speaks the words. Circumstances surrounding human beings can even be controlled by the tongue and many believers do what we call spiritual execution of their lives everyday. A certain American preacher would usually say, "Your miracle is in your mouth." And when you check the scriptures, you will find this to be true. The Bible says "With the heart a man believes but with the mouth confession is made unto salvation." But when the mouth that should bring forth the miracle is in bondage, how will the miracle happen? A lot of sisters could still have been in their husband's houses if they could control their tongues. A lot of homes would still be together if some husbands and wives were a little bit careful with their tongues. A lot of people insist on speaking out their minds. There is nothing wrong with this but when the mind is not renewed by the word of God and not washed by the blood of the Lamb, then you will get into serious trouble.

Let us examine some scriptures:

Psalm 34 verses 11 to 13 gives the prescription for long life, and that is, by keeping the tongue from evil and the lips from speaking guile. So, the fear of the Lord starts from the tongue. Proverbs 13 verse 3 tells us that, "He that keepeth his mouth keepeth his life, but he that openeth wide his lips shall have destruction." Good use of the tongue will enable us to see good days, and misuse of the tongue will lead to destruction.

Beloved, the tongue has destroyed so many things. This is why baptism in the Holy Spirit is vital and necessary for every believer. When you receive the baptism of the Holy Spirit, your tongue automatically comes under the control of the Holy Spirit. This is good for you, because whatever your tongue says will eventually happen to you. Does your tongue need deliverance? You will know by the time you finish reading this.

1

SIGNS THAT
A TONGUE NEEDS
DELIVERANCE

1. **Excessive talking:** Proverbs 10 verse 19 tells us that **"In the multitude of words, there wanteth not sin: but he that refraineth his lips is wise"** When you talk at the rate of 300 words per minute, and not willing to listen to other people, then your tongue needs deliverance.

2. **Speaking idle or careless words:** When you utter idle and useless words, it is a sign that your tongue needs deliverance.

3. **Gossiping and tale bearing:** A gossip is the devil's broadcasting station. Even if it is only your spouse you are telling the gossip, it is still gossip and you are a broadcaster for satan.

4.   **Lying.**   Proverbs 12 verse 22 says, **"Lying lips are abomination to the Lord: but they that deal truly are his delight."** When you tell lies, no matter how little, your lips are an abomination to God. A business lie or any lie at all, told for whatever reason is still a lie.

5.   **Hastiness in speech:** Proverbs 29 verse 20 says, **"Seest thou a man that is hasty in his words? There is more hope of a fool than of him."** The Bible says in this passage that there is more hope for a fool than a hasty talker. Moses was once hasty in his speech and that cost him entrance into the promised land. Psalms 106 verses 32 and 33 tells the story of Moses. It says, **"They**

angered him also at the waters of strife, so that it went ill with Moses for their sakes. Because they provoked his spirit, so that he spake unadvisedly with his lips." This put Moses in trouble. This was the man that spoke to God face to face.

6. **Swearing and cursing:** Once you swear and curse, you have a serious problem and you really need to repent. If you still use your tongue to curse and swear, it means that your tongue is glued to the chain of the enemy. There are some believers who speak the languages of hell fire. Their tongues are in bondage. For example, they call human beings created in God's image all sorts of names such as bush meat, chick, etc. You

cannot be using the devil's vocabulary and expect miracles to happen. You cannot be uttering self destructive statements such as "I am dead," "I am finished," "I am undone," or singing the devil's songs or saying the devil's prayer points (curses), and still expect good things to happen in your life. You cannot be using your tongue to extort money from people and expect God's blessing.

7. **If you have learnt or memorized incantations before, your tongue needs deliverance:** The more you recite the incantations, the more your tongue comes under bondage. If you have recited Psalms or prayed to angels as instructed by some false prophets, your tongue would be under

bondage and would need deliverance, because you have used it to pray to strange gods. Demons too can live on the tongue and this is why some people find it difficult to receive baptism of the Holy Ghost. This is why some people cannot flow in speaking with other tongues and it is also the reason why some people speak in demonic tongues. Some men got demons on their tongues by licking the sexual organs of women, and some women too got demons on their tongues by licking the sexual organs of men. This is what some people call oral sex, such tongues are in trouble. Those who have drank concoctions, demonic holy water or eaten sacrifices or kissed demonic men or women, or shared cigarettes with people, etc have their tongues under bondage. Such people tell lies without realizing it. They speak bad and filthy language easily. They utter unclean words and find it difficult to witness about Christ to anybody. They always say the negative aspect of things. They make others depressed and unhappy with their words and utterance. They speak words that put other people in bondage. They exaggerate, nag, grumble, criticize, and mock people. Many homes would have still been together if not for the power of the tongue that has destroyed them.

Healing is needed for so many tongues. Deliverance is needed for many tongues and sometimes fingers have to be laid on people's tongues to get them delivered. You too can pray to deliver yourself from this bondage, but you have to be truthful to yourself. If you know that your tongue is not speaking the right thing, accept that it needs to be delivered, and pray accordingly. It does not matter whether you are a church leader or you teach others the Bible; be truthful to yourself. One of the basic factors of life which many people do not know is that one will eventually get what one's mouth says. If you say I can, then you will. If you say I cannot, then you will not be able to do it. If you talk negatively, then you will get a negative result, because your words will of necessity create a negative atmosphere and this negative atmosphere will be hospitable to negative reactions. Try and experiment this. Determine within yourself that you will speak only positive and hopeful things for the next forty-eight hours about your job, academic performance, health, future, business and everything about your life. This may be difficult at first, because negative speaking and complaining have been programmed into the lives of so many people. If you practise speaking only positive things for seven days nonstop, you will be surprised at what will happen.

A perfect man is one who can rule his tongue. The influence of the tongue is so high that the Holy Spirit desires to use it. If you can control your tongue, then you can tame the other parts of your body. This is why you must check what you are saying. You must check to whom you are speaking, how you speak, when you speak and where you speak. When you lose the control of your tongue, you will also lose the control of your life. Therefore, the key to a beautiful life is to control and regulate your tongue. Prophet Isaiah got a vision that he was dwelling among people with unclean lips and an angel had to take a hot coal of fire from the altar and put it on his tongue to purge it. Before then, something was wrong with the tongue of prophet Isaiah, and he could not represent God until his tongue was cleansed. This is why some people prophesy and yet they still utter unprintable words with their mouths. When God wanted to judge the people at the tower of Babel, all He needed to do was to confuse their tongues, so that they could not work together again. When God also wanted to send the Holy Spirit, He also used the tongues.

The full impact of the tongue on our lives is yet to be realized, even by Christians. It is your tongue, more than anything else that determines whether you are beautiful or ugly, rich or poor.

The tongue can give delight, it can make a plain person beautiful, and it can heal bruises and wounds. It can soothe the agitated temper. The Bible says that a soft answer turneth away wrath, but when there is an exchange of hard or hot words, wrath will increase and the devil will take the advantage to create big problems. The tongue can give hope to the hopeless and point the way to God. It can make or break marriages or other situations. It can make your home a paradise or desert, make or break your children, help keep your friends or lose them, can defend a good cause or allow an evil cause to go unchecked, can heal a church or kill it, can attract people to Christ or send them away from Him. The tongue can honour God or curse God; it can also drive people to self destruction. Therefore, your spiritual reputation can largely be established by the use of your tongue. Your tongue will label your character.

2

TAMING OF THE TONGUE

Your tongue can be tamed. Here are some suggestions:

1. First of all, send your tongue for deliverance.

2. Bring it under the control of a greater power.

When the Holy Spirit descended, the first port of call was the tongue. There are only two types of tongues; clean and unclean. When it is unclean, deliverance is to apply the spiritual toothpaste of the Holy Spirit to clean it up. I have described the unclean tongues. How do we know the clean tongues? To know whether you have an unclean tongue, you must know what a clean tongue is.

Here are some qualities of a clean tongue:

A clean tongue will exercise what is known as profitable silence. A clean tongue keeps quiet when it should be quiet. The Bible says there is a time and season for everything under the sun; there is a time to keep silence (Ecclesiastes Chapter 3 verse 7). However this has been turned upside down because we talk when we should be silent and keep quiet when we should talk. The Bible enjoins us to be quick to hear and slow to speak But this also has been reversed because many people are slow to hear and quick to speak, thereby doing the direct opposite. The truth is this: if you are quiet, nobody can quote you or repeat what you said because you did not say anything.

A clean tongue does not gossip. The Bible tells us that both speech and anger are tied together. You will discover that when people get angry, they speak more rapidly. There was a lady who needed to get married and she tried all manner of things so that she could get married but failed. She even washed her head with demonic water, so that she could attract suitors but that too did not work. She tried horoscopes, it did not work. She tried the white garment churches, red garment churches, purple garment churches, etc, but none worked. Then she started attending parties and at these parties she made sure she sat close to men who looked like bachelors. That effort also failed. After some time she started making up heavily to attract attention to herself. This too did not work. She then blamed her stepmother, her own mother and everyone for her misfortune. But one day, she came to a place where she was asked to pray that God should show her the secret of her problem. After praying, she got a revelation: on a black board placed in front of her was written "ANGER" This has been her problem all the while. She had met so many men, but could not sustain a relationship with any because of her bad temper and nagging attitude. This attitude in her scared all her suitors away. She resorted to aggressive prayers, and that still did not solve her problem. He tongue needed to be delivered so that it could stop responding to the spirit of anger. When people get angry, they speak thoughtlessly. When the disagreement is over, the harsh words that were spoken during the disagreement now leave a scar. Prayer too is a two-way conversation. When you talk to the Lord, you have to listen to what He has to say.

A clean tongue is addicted to witnessing. It is always ready to speak for Christ, anywhere, and under any situation.

A clean tongue is appreciative. The story of the ten lepers in Luke 17 reflects this.

Only one of the ten lepers came back to show appreciation to Jesus. The tongue that is appreciative receives additional blessings. If you are always praising God like the Psalmist, then you are showing appreciation.

A clean tongue will speak clean words and reverence God.

Clean tongues will not speak dirty and unclean languages that should not come from the mouth of a Christian.

A clean tongue must be kind. In 1 Corinthians 13:1, we are told that a good Christian life without love is like a noisy gong or a clanging cymbal.

A clean tongue must promote peace and not unrest. You should not aggravate tempers when they are already high by adding your negative words to create more problems.

A clean tongue does not gossip. If you do not want to gossip again in your life, there is a simple rule you must obey: Anything you want to say about someone, which you cannot repeat it before him/her just let it die as stillborn inside you, do not say it. When anger dies stillborn, it will not use you, but if you give it free expression all the time, then it will use you regularly.

A clean tongue must be truthful, not one that will tell half truth or exaggerate.

A clean tongue does not grumble or complain. With a clean tongue the answer is either yes or no.

A clean tongue will make positive confessions. If as a Christian, you are always in doubt, it will conquer you. If you talk failure, it will conquer you. If you talk sickness, it will conquer you. If you talk weakness, you will receive it. If you talk poverty, you will move in and out of poverty. If you talk fear, it will grip you. If you talk bad about your marriage, the marriage will even become worse. We should not use our tongues to glorify bad situations in our lives or invite bad things into our lives.

Any Christian who wants to become a student in the school of maturity should read the book of James thoroughly and use it as a mirror to look at his or her own life. James laid emphasis on the problem of the tongue. He says if a man is unable to control his tongue, then such a man will be unable to control any other member of his body, and his religion is also in vain. You need to pray to God and you must be sincere with yourself. Some people do not use their tongues to attack others, rather they use it to attack themselves. They wage active war against themselves. It can be very sad, when you pray to God fervently to avenge you of your adversaries, and God looks down from heaven and finds out that you are your own adversary. The Bible says that by the words of your mouth you are justified and by the same word of your mouth, you are condemned. The tongue can drag one into hell fire, and it will in itself burn in hell fire.

POWER AGAINST
VERBAL DISEASES

To understand the relevance of this topic, we would consider some scriptures: 2 Kings 2:23-24 points to the experience of Elisha after he had received a double portion of the Holy Spirit. It says, "And he went up from thence unto Bethel: and as he was going up by the way, there came forth little children out of the city, and mocked him and said unto him, Go up, thou bald head, go up, thou bald head. And he turned back, and looked on them and cursed them in the name of the Lord. And there came forth two she bears out of the wood and tare forty and two children of them"

In the foregoing, we can see that those children were destroyed by the power of spoken words. Why was it this serious? If you are a good student of the Bible, you would discover that sometimes, God took some urgent steps such as the execution of people. Whenever that happened, you would find that those affected must have broken a fundamental divine law. The children in the above story mocked Elijah before he went up by the chariot. When Elisha came up, they started mocking him as well. They said to him, "Your master has gone into the skies. you too, go up." They did not stop at that. They mocked him, calling him a baldhead. We need to remember that those children were from Bethel. Bethel used to be the house of God. But one king called Jeroboam took over and converted it to a place of idolatry. He put an idol there and declared, "Behold Israel your god that delivered you from Egypt," and people were going there to worship. So, these children were polluted and the pollution spread to their mouths and put them in divine trouble.

Words are vehicles of power. If the whole of the human race was dumb, there would be no war because there would be no mouth to declare it. It is often said that, old men declare war but the young men fight it.

Those who declare war sit comfortably somewhere while others fight it.

There are three kinds of words in the Bible:

1.   Words that carry positive powers. These are divine words.

2.   Words that carry negative powers. These come from evil inspiration.

3.   Neutral words. These ones can carry positive or negative power but usually they carry no power.

Words are so powerful that the Bible has the following to say in Psalm 19:14: **"Let the words of my mouth and the meditation of my heart be acceptable in thy sight, O**

Lord, my strength, and my redeemer." It means that some words are acceptable to God while some are not.

Job 4:4 says "Thy words have upholden him that was falling, and thou hast strengthened the feeble knees." They are words of power to uphold those that are falling and to strengthen the weak.

Job 8:2 says, "How long wilt thou speak these things? And how long shall the words of thy mouth be like a strong wind?" So words can be like a strong wind blowing things up and down. Job 19:2 says, "How long will ye vex my soul and break me in pieces with words?

And Psalm 138:2 says, "I will worship toward thy holy temple and praise thy name for thy lovingkindness and for thy truth: for thou hast magnified thy word above all thy name."

God raises His words above His name. Proverbs 18:4 says, "The words of the man's mouth are as deep waters, and the wellspring of wisdom as a flowing brook." That is describing the words of man. It is as deep waters. Our Lord and Saviour, being a straight-forward, blunt speaking person, says in Matthew 12:37: "For by thy words thou shalt be justified and by thy words thou shall be condemned." He says further in Matthew 24:35: "Heaven and earth shall pass away, but my words shall not pass away." These scriptures and many more establish the fact that this is a very serious matter.

The Bible talks about the importance of words. It talks about right words, vain words, words without knowledge, false words, pure words, angry words, roaring words, words of iniquity, devouring words, selfish words, smooth words and bitter words. It also talks about words of hatred, flattering words, and swift words, which are words uttered without thinking about them. It also talks about words of wisdom and knowledge, pleasant words, wounding words and pursuing words. Proverbs 19:7 says, "All the brethren of the poor do hate him, how much more do his friends go far from him? He pursueth them with words, yet they are wanting to him." The Bible talks about words that pursue, words of faith and enticing words. In the New Testament, we read about hard words, unspeakable words and wholesome words. All these are in the Word of God to show us the importance of words.

Sometimes, we come under verbal attacks. Every sound Christian should know what to do under such a circumstance. The adverse effect of negative words on any person cannot be quantified and there is hardly anyone in this part of the world who has not been verbally harassed by somebody one way or the other. Haman used words against Mordecai. He plotted against Mordecai and Mordecai was arrested and by the same words too, Mordecai was released.

A cruel word may start a quarrel or a fight. A cruel word spoken to a person also may completely wreck the person's life. A brutal word that you speak to somebody can kill him but gracious words can smoothen the way for people. Loving words can heal and bless. In essence, the Bible makes us to understand that the words we speak hold some great values both for ourselves and those that are hearing us. It is unfortunate that we do not give sufficient attention to our words. They have the ability to bless or curse.

THE POWER IN WORDS

Words can turn situations against us or for us. The words we speak have power to clarify or confuse things and can bring light or darkness to a place. When you write down words, ensure that you write down the truth. We need to note that God stands by His own words and also by our own words. Another great truth we should note is that satan and his demons have the ability to pick up our words and work with them. The devil has no creative power. It is the words you speak that give him the power to work against you. The effect of negative spoken words can be devastating. Therefore, you need to be careful with what you listen to and what you say with your mouth.

Christians have to be careful about the kind of music they listen to because music can use words to pollute, to bless or to curse. One of the best selling records in the whole world was one song entitled, "My good Lord, my good Lord, Alleluia" In the song, the singer quietly slots in the name of a highly occult man, and people were singing and dancing to it. That kind of music can pollute people's lives. In the Yoruba culture, when a person is born, the family may decide to compose a foundational poem for him to eulogise him. If you have such a thing, I suggest you check out the words of the poem thoroughly. There was a sister who came for prayers for several months and her situation did not change. One day, God ministered to the man of God to ask her to recite this poem. She knew it offhand because her parents read it to her every morning. As she was reciting it, the man of God noticed that there was a particular line which says, "The trees in your family do not grow old." So, he asked her if they experience sudden death in her family and she said, "Yes, out of 16 children, only 4 of us are alive." The pastor said, "And they recite this to you everyday and you are rejoicing and dancing."

Words can change the course of our lives completely. Ask yourself the following questions. :hen last did you say something untrue against somebody? When last did you say something unkind about somebody else? When last did you run somebody down by what you said about him? When last did you verbally lash out at somebody in boiling anger? When last did you regret something you said? When last did you help spread a gossip? When last did you backbite? When last did you use God's name to swear? When last did you use the name of God in vain? When last did you rain abuses and curses on someone? As a parent, when last did you call your children derogatory names? Think about it.

Jesus said when you call somebody an idiot, you are in danger of judgment. When last did you enter into a shouting match with somebody and refused to keep quiet even when you were pleaded with to stop? When last did you fire an acidic arrow at your husband or wife because you were provoked? When last did you grieve the Holy Spirit by disobeying His command? Think about it. An old white man once said that the most harmful thing in the world is the tongue. He also said that the most powerful weapon in the world is the tongue. Unlike other instruments that we use, the tongue grows sharper with constant use. It is only a small part of the body but it can do enormous damage. It causes us more trouble than any other thing, Words can be tragically destructive. Unless many present-day Christians receive the divine coal of fire on their tongues, they will continue to hurt rather than heal.

Our words can destroy our relationship with God and those around us. Our words can even destroy our relationship with ourselves. So, the tongue is like having a bomb inside the house. When you look closely at the Word of God, you will discover that all creations were brought into being by God's word. The Bible says, He commanded and it came to pass. It says, "Let there be light and there was light." God gave us the power to speak. He gave us His authority and creative ability. So, we should be careful how we use this power.

Look at what Jesus said in Matthew 12:33: "Either make the tree good, and his fruit good or else make the tree corrupt and his fruit corrupt; for the tree is known by his fruit." Verse 35 says, "A good man out of the good treasure of the heart bringeth forth good things; an evil man out of the evil treasure bringeth forth evil things." So, Jesus relates our words to a tree and a fruit. The heart is the tree and the mouth is the fruit. A tree is known by its fruits; therefore what comes out of your mouth is an indication of what is in your heart. There is no question of "It just jumped out." No, what comes out of your mouth is an indication of what is in your heart.

5

EVIL TONGUES

L et us look at some of the evil tongues that the Bible talks about.

1. Undisciplined tongue. This is the type of tongue that can say anything without caring about the consequence. People with this type of tongue should pray for the coals of fire of God to come upon their tongues.

2. Unsympathetic tongues.

3. Fearful tongues.

4. Aimless tongues. Those with this type of tongue talk without a focus.

5. Unpredictable tongues.

6. Impatient tongues.

7. Proud tongues.

8. Argumentative tongues.

9.   Repetitious tongues.

10. Unaffectionate tongues.

11. Inconsistent tongues: These say one thing today and another thing tomorrow.

12. Compromising tongues.

13. Revengeful tongues.

14. Tactless tongues - tongues without wisdom.

15. Disorganized tongues.

16. Stubborn tongues.

17. Suspicious tongues.

18. Critical tongues.

19. Restless tongues.

20. Domineering tongues.

21. Talkative tongues.

22. Loud tongues.

23. Rash tongues.

These kinds of tongues and many more have landed many believers in hell fire and stolen the blessings of many.

It has been said that the best marriage is the marriage in which the wife is deaf and dumb and the husband is blind. So, the woman will not be able to talk rubbish and the man will not see rubbish. So, there will be no fight.

You can consciously or unconsciously cage your life by your words. A lot of people are labouring under what they have constructed with their mouths.

6

SOME DESTRUCTIVE
VERBAL DISEASES

Let us look at some verbal diseases that have destroyed many:

1. **Gossip:** Gossip, rumour and slander are a triplet that can destroy people. All gossips are broadcasting stations of the enemy. All gossips and backbiters are deliverance candidates. Both the gossip and the listener will face judgment. It is better to pray for people instead of gossiping about them. If you are a true child of God, gossip will not bother you. In fact, it is a fertilizer for the children of God. I rejoice when people talk about me because it means that I am important. Satanic broadcasting is a very dangerous activity. It is also very dangerous to gossip about the men of God because their

anointing and angels will deal with you. This rule is ever true: If a person gossips to me, he will gossip about me. The important thing is not to listen.

What is slander? It is an open, intentional sharing of damaging information, and the Bible condemns it. Leviticus 19:16 says, "Thou shall not go up and down as a talebearer among thy people." That is it. The Bible is against it. I Timothy 5:13 says, "And withal they learn to be idle, wandering about from house to house; and not only idle, but tattlers also and busybodies, speaking things which they ought not." Jeremiah 18:18 says, "Then said they, Come, and let us devise devices against Jeremiah; for the law shall not perish from the priest, nor counsel from the wise, nor the word from the prophet. Come, and let us smite him with the tongue, and let us not give heed to any of his words." It means that we must desist from gossiping.

2. Lying: Proverbs 6:16-19 says, "These six things doth the Lord hate: yea, seven are an abomination unto Him; a proud look, a lying tongue, and hands that shed innocent blood. An heart that deviseth wicked imaginations, feet that be swift in running into mischief. A false witness that speaketh lies, and he that soweth discord among brethren." Lying is among the seven

things that God hates. It is interesting to note that out of these seven things hated by God, nos two, six and seven have to do with the tongue. Proverbs 12:22 hit the nail on the head by saying, "Lying lips are an abomination to the Lord." The word abomination is the strongest word to describe something that God hates. Its means that Christians must speak the truth always regardless of the cost. One man said sin has many tools but a lie is the handle that fixes all the tools. When you lie against the truth, you are trailing satan's footsteps. Satan tells lies and will always like us to tell lies. When we tell lies, we support him according to John 8:44 where Jesus told some people that they are children of their father the devil who is a liar from the beginning. So, any falsehood at all is the devil's language and the language of the world. Satan promotes falsehood and lying, whether it is lying to cover up fornication, adultery or to deceive for monetary purpose or bearing false witness. A lie is a lie because it is the opposite of the truth. Some people tell lies quite easily. They have what you call the anointing of lying. When they start, you will be enjoying the lies. Yet, it is all lies. The problem about lying is that you could build a 20 storey house with lies but a word of truth would destroy it in one day. A liar may run for 50 years but truth will catch up within one second.

3. Negative confession: In Matthew 27:25, the Jews issued curses on themselves: "Then answered all the people, and said, His blood be on us and on our children." Pilate wanted to set Jesus free but they refused and said, "Let His blood be upon us and upon our children." It is still so now; no peace yet in Israel. Negative speaking is what you can call respectable sin that many do not consider to be very sinful. When somebody says, "Oh my poor leg, my poor back or my migraine," it is negative speaking. Some people would say, "Well, I was enjoying it, I knew that it was too good to be true."

Some brethren and I prayed for three sisters to receive the baptism in the Holy

Spirit at a vigil. We prayed for the first one and she started speaking in tongues. We prayed for the second one and she too started speaking in tongues. When we got to the third sister, we prayed for a long time but she did not receive. Then after some time, she looked at us and said, "Ah, it is when it comes to the toothless that eating bone becomes a problem." Then I said, "Who is the tootheless?" She said, "You can see, I have been here for one hour, it is always the pattern. Everybody will get something but when it comes to my turn, I will not get it. This is why I am not receiving it." That is negative confession when some people are doing anything, all they are waiting for is for something to go wrong and they would say, "I always know that something is going to go wrong." Negative confession. Some people make some seeming innocent statement which are very powerful. When I was in England, I used to know somebody from Zimbabwe. Anytime you said, Good morning to him, he would say, "The struggle continues." But when things began to happen, we advised him to stop talking that way. A person would open his mouth and say about his/her marriage, "I knew that this marriage would not work. I just knew it. Something has been telling me that it would not work." So many people dig their own graves with their mouths and when they come to the church, they hide the spades behind their back because at the church, they cannot say what they say at home. Remember the 12 spies who were sent to check out the Land of Canaan. They were supposed to be men of courage, valour and brilliance but only two of them, Caleb and Joshua, came back with positive reports. Others saw giants and said, "We are not able to enter, we cannot take it. We are like grasshoppers." God said, "Okay, since you said you are like grasshoppers, then you shall be grasshoppers." So, they destroyed their destiny with their own mouths.

Many years ago, I was part of a panel of interview for those who were looking for jobs. A lady who came for the interview was asked four questions and she could not answer any. When she was asked the fifth one, she said, "There is no point, after all I have already failed four. Let me pack my certificate and go." Then somebody among the panel said, "Do you know what we are writing down here?" She said, "I do not have to know. It is 4-0 already." That was how she wrote herself off. People seal their destiny with their mouths.

4. Boasting and flattering: Boasters praise themselves. They boast about their accomplishments. Unfortunately, many men of God have been destroyed by flattery. Boasting is usually a promotion of nothingness

or vanity. There is a difference between somebody telling you: "Oh, we thank God for what He is doing through you," and for another person to say, "Oh, give him a round of applause," or "welcome this great man of God to the microphone." The first one is a compliment; the second one is flattery because before God no man is great. Our compliments should be given to God.

5.   **Talkativeness:** Proverbs 10:19 says, "In the multitude of words there wanteth not sin but he that refraineth his lips is wise." Ecclesiastes 5:3 says, "For a dream cometh through a multitude of business and a fool's voice is known by a multitude of words." As far as the Bible is concerned,

a talkative is a fool. A restless tongue indicates a restless heart. Somebody who speaks without thinking is like somebody shooting without aiming. A man once said, "Don't use a gallon words to express a spoonful of thought." He also said, "The more the words that are said, the more the words that are available to be questioned. It is better to be brief and straight forward." The Bible says, **"Seest thou a man that is hasty in his words? There is more hope of a fool than of him"** (Proverbs 29:20). Let the Holy Ghost direct you before your mouth begins to speak. It helps. Do not immediately say everything in your mind the moment you feel so because to do so can be very dangerous. Moses made the mistake. He was hasty in speech and God dealt with him.

6. Immoral speech: If a person's mind is filled with dirty things, the person will speak immoral words without even thinking about it. Vain words should not come out of the mouth of a Christian, as they have no place in a Christian's life.

7. Swearing and curses: The Bible is so much against this that Matthew 5:33-36 says, **"Again, ye have heard that it has been said of men of old times, thou shall not forswear by thyself but shall perform unto the Lord thy oath. But I say unto you, swear not at all, neither by heaven (God's throne), nor by the earth, for it is his**

footstool; neither by Jerusalem. For it is the city of the great King, neither shall thou swear by your heads because thou cannot make one hair white or black." Do not curse, that is what the Bible says.

8. Using God's name in vain: Exodus 20:7 says, "Thou shalt not take the name of the Lord thy God in vain: for the Lord will not hold him guiltless that taketh his name in vain." This means using God's name as if it has no worth or value. When you use God's name in an empty and negative way, you are degrading God. So all the expressions such as: "Oh God," when there is nothing relevant, makes you guilty. Immediately a small thing happens to some people, they

would shout: "My Lord!" Nowadays, even the expression, "Praise the Lord," has been bastardized. We must be very careful the way we use God's name.

7

SOLUTION

WHAT IS THE WAY OUT?

1.   Recognise that a sick tongue is a problem of the heart. The mouth is just the barometer of the mind. It is the heart you should address. Correct it and make your mouth say better things. If you have a verbal disease, your heart needs to be cleansed by the blood of Jesus and sanctified by the word of God.

2.   Confess your sins and ask for cleansing and forgiveness.

3.   Resist evil and yield to God. That is, withdraw your tongue from the grip of the devil.

4.   Determine by the help of the Holy Spirit to use your tongue aright.

5.   Let your mouth be filled with praises to God always. It is very difficult for somebody who is using his mouth to praise the Lord always to be issuing curses and abuses.

6.   Be broken. When somebody offends you, call the person and tell him. The Bible says, "If he will not listen to you, tell the elders about it to tell him." If he would not listen, then report to the church. It is wrong to teach women to do fire for fire with their husbands. Christians should be willing to apologise when they are wrong. Even when you are right sometimes, if apology will bring peace, let peace reign.

This matter has destroyed many homes, many things and many children. When a mother calls her child a bastard, then the child will behave exactly like one. Her husband who is the father of that child may get affected too and will treat the child as a bastard by running away and not looking after him. The mother started it by calling the child a bastard.

Dear reader, if you have not given your life to Christ, prayers will not be beneficial to you. You have to be born again. This is the first step to your deliverance. A lot of problems have been dragged into many lives by the wrong use of the tongue. Many people just let their tongues loose and do not realize that it is the same tongue which they use to pray that they also use to cancel their miracles. Please pray with holy anger and determination in your spirit to deliver your tongue from satanic bondage.

Anywhere and anyway you have misused your tongue, whether consciously or unconsciously, you need to cry unto the Lord God because without that confession and forgiveness, you cannot break evil powers. Anyone you have bound with your mouth, loose him or her, in the name of Jesus.

PRAYER POINTS

1. I break the power of any evil word uttered against me, in the name of Jesus.

2. I release myself from conscious or unconscious self-imposed curses, in the name of Jesus.

3. O Lord, let not my mouth push me into hell fire, in the name of Jesus.

4. Let every satanic anchor working against me be roasted, in the name of Jesus.

5. Let the coals of fire fall upon my tongue now, in the name of Jesus.

6. Anyone I have hurt with my mouth, be released now, in the name of Jesus.

7. Oh Lord, promote me from minimum to maximum, in the name of Jesus.